Blogging for Profit

The Complete Guide to Blogging

(How to Create a Profitable Blog and Make Serious Money Online)

Table of Contents

The author of this book has taken careful measures to share vital information about the subject. May its readers acquire the right knowledge, wisdom, inspiration, and succeed.

Introduction

Congratulations on downloading this book and thank you for doing so.

The following chapters will teach you everything that you need to know about blogging, as well as how you can rake in serious money with it. Uncover the secrets of blogging, and be sure to come up with a blog that can bring in regular income.

Chapter 1 discusses the basics of blogging so that you will have a better understanding of what blogging is.

Chapter 2 talks about the ways you can monetize your blog. This is how you can turn your blog into a money-making machine.

Chapter 3 discusses the ways on how you can generate and increase traffic to your blog. As you may already know, having a high traffic is a key to blogging success.

Chapter 4 lays down the best practices that you should know, which can help guarantee your success.

Chapter 5 reveals the common pitfalls that every blogger faces. It is good for you to be aware of these pitfalls and blunders so that you can avoid committing the same mistakes.

There are plenty of books on this subject on the market; thanks again for choosing this one! Every effort was made to ensure it is full of as much useful information as possible. Please enjoy!

Chapter 1: Blogging Basics

A blog is like a personal diary that you share online. It is a special place to express your thoughts, joys, and sadness to people. It can be whatever you want it to be. Many bloggers who enjoy traveling write travel blogs. They write about their good and bad experiences, the do's and don'ts of traveling, among others. Other bloggers write about their experiences in love and in losing someone, and so much more. This is one of the best things about having a blog. You can literally share and write about anything that you want.

A blog is a very powerful tool nowadays to help reach out to people and inform them about certain things. What is more, blogging is not only a place where you can share your passions and meet people with the same interests, but it can also make you earn money. In fact, many successful bloggers earn a full-time income simply by blogging.

How to create a blog

Creating a blog is easy and simple. You do not need to learn complex codes like HTML. It is also not expensive. Just stick to the key steps revealed in this book and you will have a brand-new blog in no time.

Step 1: Decide which blogging platform you should use

When you make a search online, you will find different platforms available. The problem here is, with so many blogging platforms, how can you tell the one that best suits your needs? There are certain criteria and standards to look for. If you are knowledgeable about computer programs and codes then the best one to use is WordPress. WordPress is used by professionals worldwide, including best-selling authors. One of the best things about WordPress is that it will allow you to take full control of your blog by customizing every detail of your website. However, if you do not have adequate knowledge of computers, and if you are not willing to spend enough time to learn even the basic HTML codes, you might find Blogger as the best blogging platform for you. Blogger offers a highly intuitive user interface. It will allow you to post a new article, redesign your blog, and develop the overall layout of your website by following the simple instructions found on its platform.

There are other blogging platforms that you can find online, but WordPress and Blogger remain to be the key players in the blogging industry. Another thing to look for when deciding on which blogging platform to use is the credibility, as well as how established a certain platform is. Otherwise, you may run the risk of having a blogging platform that can suddenly close down at any time.

Step 2: Blog hosting

If you just want to blog as a hobby, then you can host your blog using a free blogging platform. However, if you are serious about blogging and want to rake in some serious profits, then you should host your own blog. Hosting a blog is easy and very affordable. There are many services online for blog hosting; one of the most recommended is BlueHost. BlueHost is a good choice especially when you use WordPress as your blogging platform. In fact, WordPress itself promotes BlueHost.

By hosting your own blog, you get to own a space on the Internet that you can rightfully call your own. In fact, this is one of the advantages of hosting your own domain. You can also customize the name of your blog without having a sub-domain, like .blogspot or .wordpress, which can make your site unprofessional.

Step 3: Domain name

Deciding on what domain name to use for your blog is important. Naming a blog is like naming a person; therefore, you need to be careful with this step. Ideally, your domain name must have a word that will reflect or describe what your blog is about, so that people will get an idea of what to expect from your blog. For example, if you are blogging about cars, then you can use the word car as part of your domain name. In fact, this is one of the techniques to increase your SEO ranking. Of course, this rule is subject to a few exceptions. There are successful bloggers who simply use their name or even a pen name yet still earn a good amount of profit from blogging. There is really no hard and fast rule to blogging. The blogging industry continues to evolve just like any other business, and so every blogger who is serious about getting a positive return should match up with the changing time and the high competition in this industry.

Step 4: Customizing your blog

Once you have opened an account with a blogging platform and have hosted your own blog, you can start uploading content on your blog. However, before you upload any content, you should first customize the layout and design of your blog. If you are using Blogger, you will have fewer problems because Blogger already has pre-set themes and designs that you can apply to your blog with just a few clicks of a mouse. WordPress is also similar; however, it is a bit more complicated than blogger.

Before you start posting content on your blog, you should customize your site by adjusting its design or layout. A good way to do this is by applying a template. Now, there are many templates that you can choose from. WordPress and Blogger offer free templates that you can use. However, you can also create and use your own template, or even download other available templates online.

If you use a template designed by other people, you should check the terms of use. Some templates can be used without any permission from or reference to the creator of a template, while others require that you first ask for permission or at least cite the creator of the template.

Step 5: Write posts and content

Once your blog is set up and is ready to accept new posts, then it is time for you to start adding content. When you upload any content, be sure that it is something that your readers will find informative, helpful, or at least entertaining. Therefore, do not rush about adding any content. After all, creating an article or any post of high quality normally takes time.

Simply keep adding content. Also, do not forget to answer any engagements or interactions that you may receive. If there is one thing that makes a blog different from a website, then that is the presence of interactions. While a website seems static and is rarely updated, a blog is more active and enjoys regular interactions with readers or visitors. Needless to say, interacting with your readers is an effective way to promote your blog. Just be sure to use kind words and be respectable at all times.

Step 6: Edit and improve

Ideally, you should always edit your writings before posting them. However, it is not uncommon to see mistakes that you have overlooked or even just ways to improve your content. Therefore, it is recommended that you check and examine the posts on your blog from time to time. This will allow you to correct any overlooked mistakes or simply find new ways to improve your blog.

Designing your blog

Your blog is like a store you want people to visit. It must be specially designed to attract people and make them stay. Your design must be able to showcase the image of your blog you want to convey. Pictures, links, banners, and content must be strategically and aesthetically positioned in a way that is easy to follow.

Here are some tips to design your blog:

1. Get inspirations

Observe your surroundings. Determine which colors, designs, prints catch your attention. You can also browse online to see which blog designs you are attracted to and get inspirations from them.

From these inspirations, make your own unique design that reflects yourself and what your blog is about.

2. Choose your colors sensibly

Too much is not always good. Less is more. Keep your color choices to the following: any of the main primary colors, and your go-to color. Grey is also used on professional websites. Tip: Using contrasting colors can work wonders with the right design.

Make sure they are what the majority like. There are some colors that encourage people to visit again and there are some that put off people. Every color signifies different meaning to people; so, make sure to choose color combinations that not only appeal but convey the right message to your audience.

3. White space is not always bad

Do not make the mistake of trying to fill in every portion of your blog. In fact, having white or empty spaces is recommended because it improves readability. Take note that too much of something on your site can be distracting and overwhelming to website users. You can use white spaces as borders which can help your headlines and other significant parts of your blog be more visible.

4. Your design must be goal-oriented

What is your blog for? If your main purpose is to generate sales, then you should have a catchy and professionally written sales page. However, if your objective is to convert your visitors into subscribers, whether through a newsletter or a direct email subscription, then your blog must be designed not only to persuade a visitor to sign-up but it must also make it easy and convenient to join your email list.

5. Follow conventions

Your design can be whatever you want and however you want it to be. But, if you want to assure a good user experience, make sure your blog has the following conventional features:

- Attribution to authors
- Pages
- Headers
- Search bars
- Sidebars
- Options to subscribe

These essential features help the users to easily navigate your blog. Moreover, these can help your audience effortlessly find your blog and make them stay longer.

6. Experiment

Following the norms is important in designing your blog. But, it doesn't mean you cannot try to add new features and experiment with some details of your blog.

Spice up your blog by mixing things up to create a new experience for your visitors. Just make sure it is not overwhelming for your visitors and it is still easy to find and read.

7. Make it interactive

When you blog, it is important to build a good relationship with your audience to increase the traffic to your blog. It would be better if your visitors can easily reach you by adding a comment or suggestion box on your blog. With this, they can easily react to your posts and build a connection with you by exchanging insights.

8. Use responsive web design

Responsive web design enables your page to look good on any devices (tablets, mobiles, and desktops). It can resize accordingly to the size of the screen or web browser. This approach increases the usability of your blog and increases the satisfaction of your visitors.

How to choose a profitable niche

The Internet is a big market and you have the whole world as your consumer. So, making a blog and making it a business can be your ticket to a financially stable life. With this, it is possible for you not to be trapped in a job with strict schedules and rules. You can have a high income but still be able to enjoy your life more. You have a handle of your own schedules and are able to balance having a life and having a job to your liking.

To be successful on the Internet, you need to find a niche that will give you a nice hefty income. A niche is a community you will be in and where your products and services can be offered. It is necessary for you to pick a niche that matches your passions and expertise; so, you will be able to love what you are doing and work doesn't seem to be too stressful.

It is better to have one niche for a start. Focusing on one niche gives you the concentration you need to make your blog successful. You will be able to focus on your subject well and be able to produce great content for your audiences. Accordingly, you can build more audiences and gain their trust faster. These audiences can one day become your paying customers.

Being a one-man team, you will not be overwhelmed by managing different niches at the same time; thus, increasing your productivity.

You will be able to have a low cost by starting one niche; as a result, you have a low risk. If it doesn't work out, it is easy for you to try other niches.

Choosing a niche wisely is very important. You can start by writing down a list of possible ideas for your blog and business. You can write whatever you think of. It is not needed to be rational. Feel free to explore creative and even crazy ideas.

You can write down a list of niches you are fond of visiting. Write down your interests, passions or the skills you are confident you possess. List down your hobbies and or what kind of business you want to have, lots of ideas, the better.

You narrow down your list by picking the top five ideas that match your favorite niches. Focus on ideas that you love. Make sure they are something that you really are passionate about so you can immerse yourself in turning it into a successful one. If you do not enjoy the subjects much, you will not be motivated enough to work on them.

Once you have narrowed them down, you need to determine which of them is the most profitable. You can research online. Start by typing keywords related to your niche on the Google search bar. Look for broad topics as well as the specific features of your chosen niche. It is good if there are many results online. It means it has a big market interested in the topic.

Next, do a keyword search using the services available online, like Google AdWords Keyword Planner. With this kind of service, you will be able to know the estimated number of times the keywords are searched and how the number changes in time. A good indicator of a good niche is if the main keywords you have chosen and the other related specific keywords have a high number of searches per month. This usually means that there is a big demand for this kind of niche.

You can also use Amazon to do your keywords search. You can type in the main and specific keywords in the search bar to know if there are many products related to your niche. The more results found, the bigger chance that your niche is profitable.

A way to test if your niche has a market, is to visit affiliate marketing websites. Here you can search for your niche and see if many products are available. If there are, it usually means there is a demand. You could also sell some of the products you like and earn a commission.

It might be difficult to make a business successful online if you chose a niche with a lot of competition, but a lot of competition can also mean a big market for your products and/or services. You must sell yourself and have a good marketing campaign. Pour your heart and lots of effort into your niche to be successful.

Search engine optimization

Search engine optimization or SEO is the key to blogging. If you want your blog to be found online, then you must focus on SEO. Consider the fact that there are thousands and millions of blogs online. With all these blogs, how can your blog be found? Answer: SEO.

SEO is a marketing approach that increases blog visibility. The number one thing about SEO that you should learn is the use of keywords. Using keywords in your article is what makes them easy to find by search bots. So that when someone makes a search online, your blog may be recommended on the first page of search page results. Keywords must be related to your post and should be specific. Gone are the days when you can just use one or two words as your keywords. Today, you should focus on long-tail keywords. Do not worry; this will be discussed later on in the book.

There are many things that affect the SEO ranking of a blog. Of course, the quality of your posted content is very important. Every post that you make should be informative and professionally written. Do not worry; as long as you stick to the lessons and best practices in this book, then you are on the right track.

Write or hire?

If you want to have a successful blog, then you need to fill it in with lots of high-quality content. There are two ways to create content for your blog: Ideally, you should write the content yourself. However, many people have wonderful ideas but do not know how to express them effectively in writing. In such case, you may want to hire a professional ghostwriter to turn your ideas into words.

You can easily find ghostwriters by making a search online. You can also find people who would write the content for you at a cheap price of even $3 for a 500-word article. You can find many of these writers from content mills, such as Freelancer, Guru, or even from a gig service site like Fiverr.

Take note, however, that most of those writers who agree to write articles at a cheap cost also deliver low-quality articles. To earn money, they tend to write very fast which sacrifices the quality of the work. More than 90% of writers from content mills are "writers" who really do not know how to come up with a decent article. However, if you get lucky, you may be able to find a writer who can create high-quality posts for a cheap price. But, do not expect such writers to work for you for long, because chances are that they will soon find a client who will give them a better offer. After all, good writers deserve better rates.

Again, it is best if you are also the one who do the writing for your blog. After all, it is your personal space. Writing is not hard, especially if you are writing something about you are passionate about. You do not need to be a professional writer. Just learn the basics of writing, such as the proper use of grammar and punctuations. The more you write, the better you will get good at it.

Blog vs. website

These two terms may be used synonymously. However, for the word geeks out there, a blog is more interactive than a website. It usually has space after every post where people can leave comments and interact with one another. In a way, it is less formal than a website. A blog also gets updated with new content on a regular basis. Usually, you will find new content on a weekly basis. Some bloggers update their blogs daily. This is a matter of personal preference. Just make sure that each new post that you publish on your blog is worth reading. Consequently, a website tends to be more formal and does not get updated as much as a blog. A good example of a website is a business website or an author's website. Many of these websites do not have space where a visitor can write a comment on a particular post.

Chapter 2: Monetize Your Blog

There are many people who make a lot of money from blogging. With hard work and patience, you could earn enough to cover your expenses in maintaining the blog and go on to make huge profits.

With your blog set up and traffic coming, here is a handy list on how to monetize your blog:

1. Sell your own product or service

Typically, you write topics you really are knowledgeable about on your site. So, it would be better if you are able to earn sharing your expertise by creating ebooks, and then eventually, video courses.

Selling services like writing services, consulting services, teaching services, and etc. to your audience is another good way to monetize your blog. For example, a fitness instructor can offer fitness programs on diet and exercise plans. Depending on your website, you can be more specific. How much you will charge your clients depends on you. You can do this by making automated email messages or with Skype calls.

The Internet is full of consumers. If you have a product or service, sell it online. You have the whole world to offer your product or service to.

2. Affiliate Marketing

One of the most popular ways to monetize your blogs is by promoting products or services. You earn a commission if your visitors click on your affiliate link and purchase the product or service. The commission can range from 10% all the way up to to 50% of the sale price or sometimes more.

When selecting a business' affiliate program, it is best to choose a product or service that you have used and would really recommend to your audience. Also, it is good to put a disclaimer and promote a business that is related to your website.

You can find products to promote by joining big-name programs like Amazon Associates, Clickbank and Commission junctions. Many people earn a full-time income simply by focusing on affiliate links. Be careful though, because even though expert bloggers boast about earning thousands of dollars with affiliate links, the majority of bloggers earn only pennies or even none at all. But, if you are willing to exert serious time and effort, then you should know that earning big money through affiliate links is easily doable. Just persevere and continue to observe the best practice of professional bloggers.

3. Pay per click ads

Get paid with every click on the ads of your visitors. There are many providers with this kind of service online like Chitika, Clicksor, and Bidvertiser. But the most used is Google AdSense. It is well-matched with free Blogger blogs and self-hosted WordPress blogs.

AdSense allows bloggers to place relevant ads on their websites to make money. There are lots of online advertisements to choose from. You can format them any way you want to suit your website and place them in strategic places to increase your click-through-rate. You have a control on everything.

It is free and very easy to do. You sign up and choose your ads. Copy and paste the codes and place them on your site. Then, it is a waiting game. Google will be the one to bill the advertisers and networks. The more audience you have, the better chances to get clicks.

4. Sponsored posts

If your website has a loyal audience, a good way to make money is to post product reviews on your website. You can select products from services like Tomoson, BlogPRWire, SheSpeaks, and so on.

Make sure that the product you will choose to review is something you want, something your audience will take an interest with and it must be suitable to the theme of your blog.

5. Remarketing

You can get most of the visitors on your blog by remarketing. It l you place ads in front of your targeted guest who recently visited your website as they surf the Internet elsewhere. It is a great help to advertise your product and it is not an expensive service.

6. Build an email list

A high traffic is very necessary to monetize your blog. To keep them updated about your site and your latest offerings, sending email notifications is an easy way to entice interested individuals to make a purchase. You can also monetize these email notifications by placing banner ads and affiliate links.

So, start building your email list from the start. To keep enticing readers to join, offer freebies and regularly update your blog with fantastic content your audience will love.

Availing autoresponder services like GetResponse, AWeber, Mad Mimi, and more, are very helpful if you are really serious about building your email list. Needless to say, investing in your email list can do wonders for your business. In fact, if you are serious about making money with your blog, expert bloggers would tell you to focus on building your email list. But, the question remains: How do you grow your e-mail list?

The best way to grow your e-mail list is by offering useful content on your website. Always remember that you should earn the trust of your readers. Otherwise, how can you expect for them to sign up on your e-mail list? People do not hesitate to sign up when they feel that they can trust you. To build trust, the best way to do it is by offering useful information on your blog.

7. Turn your blog into a brand

The Internet has an abundance of competition. It is very important for you to have effective branding strategies to give you a major edge.

Your blog must be designed well to define who you are and what people can expect from you. You must be able to differentiate your offerings to others to get the attention of your visitors.

Be patient in building up your blog. Not all strategies will work for you, it is all trial and error. It also takes time to monetize your blog, but with the right strategies and hard work, it can be attained quicker.

Chapter 3: Increase Your Traffic

Creating a blog about your passion or interest is easy, but many people have a hard time building and maintaining a good flow of traffic, which is essential for a successful blog. You need good strategies to have visitors on your blog and keep them coming.

1. Strategize your content

Have your website established and well-designed to attract visitors. Make sure they would enjoy staying and navigating your blog by providing them with good content. The content must be something the audience would love. It can either be entertaining or informational.

Just like in business, you need to have a feasibility study of your industry subject. You should gather information about what are the readers' frequently asked questions, what is already written about your field, and how other sites showcase their content so that you will be able to come up with better content.

You can get ideas from Quora, Buzzsumo or other blog topic generators. Make sure that your content is creative and eye-catching, as well as informational, so that people will keep coming back to your site and share your posts.

Making your content long lasting is a good way to keep your traffic. Try to create posts where time will not make them irrelevant.

Headlines of your content must be irresistible to call the attention and capture the interest of your visitors. Great posts behind inconspicuous headlines will be useless. Your readers will not even click on them. So, use headlines or titles that will be persuasive enough that when your target readers encounter your title, they will have a strong urge to learn more about what you have posted. Of course, catchy headlines are only a part of a successful blog. What will make the real sale or conversion is the substance of your content?

Be innovative with your headlines to promote your blogs. You can play about with them to see which works best. Promoting your content is another means that should be added in strategizing your content. By sending newsletters about what is new in your blog, you will be able to bring back visitors. You can also send them weekly or monthly updates of your best posts.

2. Keywords

Putting keywords and using SEO to drive traffic to your site is a must. With keywords and search engine optimization, people can easily find your site by just typing their question in their favorite search engine.
Moderately using SEO can do wonders to your blog. Using keywords can really help, but placing too many keywords can saturate the content completely with search queries.

You can also link your content to other related blog posts but be careful not to put too many links in your blog posts as too many sentences dotted with blue hyperlinks won't be appealing to the reader.

There is massive competition for popular keywords. So to have a bigger chance of being found, use long-tail keywords. Having three keywords phrases can lessen your competition.

3. Track down your audience

Promoting your blog to your target audience must be expertly planned. Below are some ideas to help get your blog out to the masses.

Research and choose which social networking sites are best suited to your blogs. Do you have lots of videos you can share? You might try posting them on Youtube. If your blog uses lots of visuals, you can maybe use LinkedIn. There are many sites to choose from to suit the style of your blog.

Identify sites that your type of audience visits. Taking into account your audience's personalities, you will be able to have referral links from significant websites.

Engage and participate in conversations where you can. Join their discussions and link and comment your blog if the opportunity allows. Try and write helpful comments and make yourself known to be someone who is very knowledgeable and valuable to your community. Through this, you can drive traffic to your blog.

Another technique is to ask your audience to share your content. But, limit your social sharing options to the networks that you think can have the biggest influence like Facebook and Twitter.

When you find the best networks that work for you, stick to them and focus on them to increase your productivity and have better results.

4. Speed up your site and go mobile

When you visit a site, you want it to load fast, if it doesn't, you are likely to go somewhere else. So, make sure your blog is up to speed. It should be able to load fast enough so the audience will not think of going to what is next on Google's list.

You can check your blog's speed with Google's Page Speed Insight tool. With this service, it can give the speed of your blog a score. If it is not up to standard, it can give you tips on what you need to boost up your blog's speed.

Nowadays, most people spend their time with their phones or tablets. It is natural to make your blog mobile friendly. There are WordPress plug-ins, among others, like WPTouch Mobile Plug-in and Jetpack by WordPress to help your blog be more mobile friendly.

5. Establish good relationships

Being nice to others is highly recommended online if you want to have more people follow you. You need to team up with co-bloggers to help promote each other.

Leave thoughtful comments on other blogs and actively involve yourself in your community. Connect yourself with other bloggers by citing their blogs and tag them to let them know. There is a big chance that they will post and mention it. You will get more shares and more traffic in return.

Chapter 4: Best Practices

Although there is no hard and fast rule to blogging, successful bloggers have certain practices in common. These are the best practices that you should observe to significantly increase your chances of success:

High-quality content

The quality of your content is vital to your success. Make sure that every article or post that you upload on your blog is of high quality. This means that there should be no grammatical errors, or they should at least be kept to a minimum. Do not worry; you do not need to be a professional writer. However, you should try to express yourself in a way that your readers will find it easy to connect and understand.

When it comes to blogging success, the content of your blog play a crucial role. All successful bloggers have good quality content on their sites. The quality of your content is also relative since it must be viewed in connection with its competitors. Even if you have an informative post, it would not be considered good if most of your competitors offer more information on their blogs. Therefore, it is helpful and practical to study and analyze the content of your competitors.

Use short paragraphs

Reading online, on a computer, or any other device is different from reading paperback books. Research shows that dividing long paragraphs into two or more smaller paragraphs can significantly enhance readability. Also, many website visitors tend to shy away from blogs that use long paragraphs. Long paragraphs simply look intimidating and difficult to read. Take note that when a person reads on a device, it puts more strain on his eyes. You can make the reading experience easier for your readers by simply using short paragraphs instead of long paragraphs that look like big blocks of texts on the screen.

Interact

Interacting with your audience is important. In fact, by simply interacting with your blog visitors, you can increase engagements and your blog traffic by more than five times. Interacting is simply replying to any comments that people may write on your posts. A simple "Thank you for the kind comment." would be very much appreciated.

Blogging is sharing. Usually, people who have the same interest as you will respond to your posts. Also, if those people have their own blogs, it would help if you also check their blogs and also give a comment. In the online world of blogging, you simply have to treat other people the way you want to be treated. It is like social media, but has a more professional approach.

There may come a time when you may receive a bad comment from a reader. When this happens, keep calm and remain professional. Do not reply in an offensive manner even if the comment appears to be rude or completely out of place. Some people may leave negative comments because that is simply how they think or feel about your blog, while others may do it simply for the sake of writing a bad comment. Either way, you should maintain professionalism. After all, if the negative comments are completely out of place, your other blog visitors will notice it and may even defend your blog for you.

When you receive a bad comment, you should keep an open mind. Consider the comment and be completely honest with yourself. If the said negative comment holds water, then make adjustments. This will make your blog better, and you may consider the said bad comment as a blessing.

Interacting is not only limited to your blog. After all, social media channels these days can easily be connected to your blog. In fact, social media is an excellent way to promote your blog and drive regular traffic. Most of the time, social media is also the key to getting your content go viral on the Internet, which brings us to the next topic.

Use social media channels

Do not underestimate the power of social media channels like Facebook, Twitter, LinkedIn, Google+, and others. Once you establish a good following on social media, you can drive a consistent flow of traffic to your blog.

If you are not a fan of social media, you can simply focus on one social media channel. After all, your readers can be the one to share your blog on their own social media, which can lead your posts to reach even other social media channels.

When it comes to blogging, Facebook and Twitter are the best social media channels to use. They are also the most famous channels for sharing anything.

Take note that when you take advantage of social media, you should follow some professional etiquette. For example, do not keep sharing new content every minute. Your followers are real people; so do not bombard them with too much information.

Make every share count. If you continue to harass your followers with lots of contens, they might unfollow you.

The element of time is also important. Find out the time when most of your connections are online so that they will easily see any new posts that you make. The exact time to post a new content is relative, depending on your location, as well as the location and behavior of your connections. By posting a new content at different times of the day or night, you will be able to identify the best time when most of your followers are online.

Use images

Seeing a site that is composed of nothing but blocks of texts may look intimidating. It gives an impression that the reader is about to engage in a hard reading session, which usually sends blog visitors away. As they say, pictures speak louder than words. You do not have to use many images. One picture per post is enough. Just make sure that the image is something that you can safely use, and that it is relevant to the topic of your post.

It is highly recommended that you use an image when you share a post via social media. Research shows that having pictures increases responses and engagement. Some people are simply too lazy to read and may not be able to realize the great information that you are sharing. However, by adding a catchy picture, they will be persuaded to know more about what you are sharing with them.

You may share an image that you have taken yourself, or you can use images of public domain. You can find many of these images online. If the image is not of public domain, be sure to ask permission from the owner before you use the image.

Grow your e-mail list

Ask any professional and successful blogger, and he will tell you that having an e-mail list is very helpful, especially if your blog is offering a product or a service. Take, for example, Amazon, from time to time it sends a copy of products that it thinks would be interesting for their subscribers. Of course, you cannot expect that 100% of those on your e-mail list will make a purchase of whatever it is that you are offering, but even if you just get 2-10% that converts into sales, it's still profit. After all, you can always send another offer later on.

Give helpful information

This is an important part of having good-quality content. This requirement cannot be overstated. By giving helpful information to your readers, you will not only receive regular visitors but you can also gain their trust, which is important to success. After all, you cannot expect anyone to purchase any goods or services on your blog if they do not trust you. In fact, they would hesitate to spend even a penny. By giving helpful information, you get to establish a relationship with your readers that is based on trust and confidence. This is another reason why you should interact with your blog visitors. Such interactions, especially if in a positive tone, builds trust.

Use Google Adsense

Among the many ways to earn profit out there through ads posted on your blog, Google Adsense is the number one choice. This is because Google Adsense is the program that offers the highest pay.

The problem most people have when it comes to Google Adsense is how to have their blog approved to display ads from Google. If you know the right steps to take, then this should not be a problem. Do not listen to articles online that emphasize how hard it is to have a blog approved for Google Adsense. By observing the best practices and lessons in this book, you can have your blog approved without an issue.

Before you apply to display Google Adsense on your blog, your blog should already be well designed and have at least 50 posts. You should already have regular visitors on your blog, and some interactions. Now, this is easy. Here is the secret: Join Google+. Google+ is the social media platform of Google where you can share your content with other people. It also has communities that you can join. Be sure to join active communities that are related to your blog's topic, and post your content there with a link to your blog. Also, it helps if you comment on other people's posts. By doing so, you will also get interactions on your own blog. Again, the golden rule applies: Do to others what you would want them to do to you.

It is worth noting that there are blogs that earn money even without any ads posted on their site. The big disadvantage of having ads on your site is that it tends to ruin the professional look of your blog. Therefore, even if your chosen method to earn money is through ads, avoid posting too many ads on your blog. Having a lot of ads ruins the reading experience, which can decrease your blog's traffic. There are people who earn a big income without advertisements; instead, they sell products or services. The most common way is to put up a blog that is full of information about a particular subject, and then offer an ebook for sale.

Use long-tail keywords

When it comes to increasing visibility online or search engine optimization (SEO), the use of long-tail keywords is the way to go. Long-tail keywords or keyword phrase refers to a group of three or more keywords. Due to the high volume of published content online, the use of simple one or two keywords is no longer recommended. For example, using a mere keyword such as "blog" is no longer recommended. Instead, you should be more specific. Example: Instead of simply using "blog" as a keyword, use "How to monetize your blog." This will increase your chances of appearing and being found when a user makes a search online related to your subject.

Identifying the right keywords to use is very important. Google Keyword Planner is helpful for this. It is also worth noting that people who make a search online do not really think too much about what they are writing in the search bar. You should keep this in mind when deciding on what keyword phrase to use. People tend to use only simple words and phrases.

Choose the right domain name

Choosing the right domain name is important. Ideally, your domain name should include a word that will describe what your blog is about. For example, if you are a travel blogger, then you might want to use the word "travel" as part of your domain name. The reason here is to give the reader an idea of what your blog is about. After all, a name should share something, and your domain name must share something about your blog. It is also worth noting that including even one keyword in your domain name is a good way to increase your SEO ranking.

Guest posting

Guest posting is an excellent way to promote your blog. Many well-established websites accept guest posts. In fact, some of them even pay more than $100 per post that gets accepted for publication on their site.

Most of the sites or blogs that accept guest posts are well-established and have thousands of visitors a day. Most of the time, they will allow you to share a link to your site — which is a great way to drive lots of traffic to your own blog.

Well-established sites usually require a high standard of content. You may write the article yourself or hire a professional ghostwriter to do the work for you. Also, before you write anything for a guest post, check the editorial guidelines for guest posting. The guidelines are usually posted on the site itself, usually under the write for us or editorial section. If nothing is stated on this matter, you could offer to guest post by contacting the site administrator through the contact us page, if any.

Have an about me page

Be more personal and let your blog visitors know who you are. People do not just like a blog because of the content, but also because of the author of the blog. If you have a naturally friendly personality, then this should not be a problem. Write something about yourself and let your readers know who you are on a personal level.

Do not make your visitors feel that they are merely dealing with some random page on the Internet. It is better if your posts makes them feel like they are really talking with a real person.

The way to do this is to introduce yourself as a person by letting them know who you are. It is also helpful to add a profile image of yourself. Just be sure that it is a decent image. The more people know about you on a personal level, the more the connection grows. This also helps to establish trust.

Use sharing buttons

Make sure that every post that you publish on your blog can easily be reshared. Many people reshare interesting things that they find online. If you know something about programming, then you can make your own reshare buttons. If not, do not worry; most blogging platforms offer reshare buttons that you can use on your blog. You can also use services like AddThis, which will provide you with sharing buttons that you can apply to your blog.

Use a simple template design

When you design your blog, you may get tempted to use templates that have wonderful designs. Although they may look good, it is suggested that you stick to simple designs. This is because having complicated designs may make your blog appear hard to navigate. Of course, this is subject to a few exceptions, especially when your blog is about website design.

Upload new content

Search engines prefer new content over old content. Therefore, you should update your blog with new content regularly. By uploading new content, your regular visitors will also have something new to read and enjoy. Also, if people know that you update your blog regularly, then they will check your blog from time to time to check for new posts. If they get to like your blog, they will not hesitate to sign up for your e-mail list or newsletter.

Quality vs. quantity

The quality of your posts is more important than the quantity. In fact, you may have a successful blog even if you just upload one article per week. However, if you only upload one article a week, it might take a long time for your blog to be well-established. It is also worth noting that although the quality of your post is more important than the quantity, it does not mean that quantity is no longer important. Remember that the more high-quality articles that you post, the more you increase your blog's visibility, which translates to more traffic and sales. Therefore, even if you place more emphasis on quality, you should also work on the quantity of your posts.

Use short and easy to remember URL

Your URL should be the name of your blog. Do not make it hard to remember. Keep it short, so that people will easily memorize it. Also, do not make it hard to spell or pronounce. You might encounter a situation where someone will ask for your blog's URL, you should be able to answer directly and clearly.

Use reputable sources

When you write non-fiction blogs like how-to guides or self-help blogs, you should use reputable sources to support your claims. This is a good way to establish more trust and also to avoid plagiarism. When citing sources, you can use the well-known styles such as APA or Chicago style referencing to a source. If this is hard for you, simply use your own style. Just be sure to cite your source properly.

Fill in the gaps within your niche

Once you have a niche, you can expect to find a number of articles written about it. However, there are many ways to tackle the same subject. A slight shift in perspective can allow you to come up with an entirely new idea. For example, instead of writing about the health benefits of tea, you can write about the superstitious beliefs that people in Japan have about drinking tea. You can also add some scientific basis to support or deny such claims.

Call to action

Use call to action messages. Astonishingly, most web users are open to suggestions. After all, just the fact that they access the web and make searches means that they are open to ideas and opinions. However, many of them need to be guided. Therefore, you should include a call to action to make their experience more convenient.

A call to action is not just about asking a visitor to buy a product or service that you offer. A call to action can be as simple as telling your reader at the end of the article to start applying the lessons he has learned right now or to click on a particular link in case he or she would want to know more about a specific subject. A call to action can also be a way to persuade a visitor to sign up for your e-mail list or newsletter.

Add ALT texts to images

Adding images is good. However, merely adding images alone will not increase your SEO ranking. In fact, it will not help you generate more visibility. The way to increase visibility with images is by adding ALT text to every image that you upload on your blog.

Without the ALT text, search engines like Google will not understand what the image is. An ALT text is simply a short description of the image. Again, do not use keyword stuffing.

Perseverance

Like anything of value, it takes time to create a well-established blog. It's likely you won't notice any developments in the first few weeks, but if you pursue the best practices and lessons in this book, you will notice some massive changes and make massive profit over time.

Blogs that earn thousands of dollars per month did not happen just by chance. They were not built in a day. In fact, many of those blogs are more than a year old. However, it is possible to earn lots of income from blogging. It is doable, and many bloggers are already enjoying such luxury of simply sharing what they love and earning a full-time income.

Improve your writing

Even if you do not consider yourself as a professional writer, it would not hurt if you try to improve your writing skills. Basic lessons on grammar and word flow will be helpful to your success as a professional blogger. In fact, if you take the time and check the blogs of top-earning bloggers, you will notice that most of them, if not all, are excellent writers. Do not worry; writing is not hard. All you need to do is to keep on writing. Simply practice, practice, and practice some more.

Study your competitors

Pay attention to blogs that have the same niche and target market as you have. Check their blogs and see if they have anything on their blogs that you have not covered. Also, pay attention to any topics within your niche that other blogs have not yet covered. Remember that there are many ways to approach a particular topic.

You can also have a mutual relationship with your competitors. Most bloggers also help promote the blogs of their competitors. By doing so, you get to have healthy competition and help each other generate more traffic.

Competition is not bad. In fact, it is what propels businesses and bloggers to improve. Many effective strategies were born out of tight competition. Instead of fighting against competition which is impossible, you should aim to turn it into your advantage.

Blog about something that you are passionate about

Blogging is a life-long journey. Although you can blog about anything that you want, and even about things that you do not know anything about (especially when you hire a ghostwriter to write the content for you), it is best to come up with a blog that you are passionate about. Even if the blog fails to make any profit, you can still be happy of all the labor that you put in your blog. Also, if you blog about something that you love, there is a good chance that you will be able to come up with helpful and meaningful content — and this is the key to success. If you look at the best earning blogs in the world, you will notice that their authors are also those who share a profound interest in the subject that they are blogging about.

Every topic in the world has a market. So, do not worry if your blog is simply about meditation or poetry. Although the market may be small for such subjects, it does not change the fact that there is an existing market for such interests. Also, who knows, if you come up with a wonderful blog, maybe even someone who does not like your subject may start to have an interest after reading the quality of your posts.

Chapter 5: Common Pitfalls and How to Avoid Them

To increase your chances of success, here are the common pitfalls that you should be aware of. Some of these have been discussed above. It is important that you pay attention to these common mistakes and blunders so that you can make the necessary adjustments, and come up with a successful blog that will bring in decent profits.

Using long paragraphs

When writing online, you should stay away from using long paragraphs. Take note that reading on a computer or any other gadget is different from reading a real paperback book. When writing online, you should cut your paragraphs. You can do this simply by dividing a long paragraph into two or more short paragraphs.

Make sure that the layout is easy on the eyes in order to enhance the reading experience. Reading using a computer or any gadget, especially for long hours, can easily strain the eyes. Long paragraphs also look intimidating. When a visitor enters your website and sees the content written in long paragraphs, it tends to discourage the reader from reading more. Instead, he will just visit another site and miss out the wonderful information posted on your site. Using short paragraphs, with each paragraph packed with useful information, is one of the keys to success when writing online.

Low-quality content

As discussed, make sure that every article or content that you post on your blog will be useful to your readers. Even if you have a thousand articles published on your blog, if the quality of those articles are not good, then you cannot expect your visitors to visit it again.

You can avoid low-quality content by making sure that every post that you make will provide your readers with as much useful information as possible. Make sure that every article or post that you make is well researched and packed with information that your readers need.

Not using images

As discussed, It is advisable to use at least one image per post on your blog. It simply looks boring to see a blog that is full of texts and nothing more.

Research shows that people tend to click content that are accompanied with an image rather than those articles shared online that are composed of pure texts.

Not interacting

Most people enjoy interacting with their blog's audience. However, there are those who get tired of all the interactions. Although interacting is not required, it is very helpful and effective in drawing more attention to your blog. Most people who regularly interact with you will take the liberty of sharing your blog. And, as you may already know, social media is an excellent tool for growing your traffic. In fact, it is the key to going viral on the Internet.

Keyword stuffing

Although keywords matter for purposes of SEO, you should not fill your content with too many keywords, especially useless keywords. Take note that search engine these days, especially Google, are much advanced than before. They will recognize if you merely stuff your content with keywords. Once Google or any other well-established engines detects that you have simply stuffed your article or any content with keywords, it will not recommend your site, which may cause a drop in your traffic and conversions.

Too many pop-ups and ads

Avoid having too many things that pop-up on your blog. And, as already mentioned, having too many ads can be a big disadvantage.

Ideally, you should have only one pop-up on your blog or none at all. Having too many will only ruin the reading experience. Take note that many web users only want to find specific information that they need. If you use many pop-ups on your site, you may end up sending many of your visitors away.

You may use a pop-up to persuade the visitor to sign up to your newsletter or e-mail list. Of course, before anyone will sign up, you should first gain their trust. Again, the way to establish trust is by sharing useful information on your blog.

Buying followers

You can find many services online that will give you tons of followers in exchange for a few bucks. Although having a high number of followers is good and demonstrates trust, if such followers are fake then you will also have low-quality connections or followers who simply do not care about what you post.

When you purchase followers, you tend to end up with fake followers, or followers who are not real humans. The big disadvantage here is having a high number of followers with little engagements on your posts. Imagine a blog that has 2,000 followers, but only 3 people interact with the new posts. How would you feel about it? Instead of wasting your money buying followers, focus on creating and sharing helpful articles and content online.

Aim to build a network of high-quality followers. These are followers who will engage with your posts and even reshare them. Although buying followers may be tempting since it is an easy way to have a blog that looks well established, it is simply not recommended. You also cannot expect to have any sales from such followers, since most of them will have a fake account that also support other blogs.

Using multiple ways to monetize your blog

Do not forget that first and foremost, a blog is a way of sharing. Obviously turning your blog into a money-making machine will be disappointing for your visitors. Although you can combine the different ways to monetize your blog, it is not good to fill your blogs with lots of ads and things for sale. It will appear to every reader that your blog is only there to make money out of them.

Your blog should be a place where you share information and things about yourself. Every post must help your visitor and create a good experience. In fact, many blogs earn with nothing more but offering a single e-book for sale on the blog.

Plagiarism

Plagiarism is not only bad for your blog, but you can also be held personally liable for it. Instead of plagiarizing, cite your sources. This is also another reason why you should write a blog on a subject that you personally know as it's easy to share your own experiences. After all, there is no plagiarism when you simply share your own honest experiences.

Rewriting other people's content

This is something that many people commit these days. This is also plagiarism. Take note that even if the content passes Copyscape Premium, it does not mean that it is already 100% free from plagiarism. Plagiarism, after all, is not about copying a particular writer and claiming it as your own. It deals with the copying of ideas and claiming them as your own. Do not re-word other people's articles. When you write something, express your own thoughts and ideas on the subject. Of course, you can use other people's ideas, just be sure to also cite the sources of those ideas.

Not thinking like a publisher

Although you are blogging and think that you can just share anything that you want, you may improve your blog's performance by thinking like a publisher. After all, once you are a blogger, you also become a publisher at the same time.

You might be wondering just how thinking like a publisher can help you be successful. Thinking like a publisher means considering what your market wants or needs to read. This is the way to come up with content that really sells and gets reshared thousands of times.

You should think of blogging as a business. The better blog posts you come up with, the more traffic you pull in which can generate more income. Publishers always mean business, and thinking like a publisher means that you should manage your blog strategically. This also means being strategic about the posts that you publish. For example, if you are blogging about life or even about parenting, you should also pay attention to the seasons and any special events that may be coming. If Easter is getting near, then you might want to start working on an interesting article on how to make Easter celebration with your kids more exciting.

Although as a blogger, you can feel free to share whatever you want, as a publisher, you should consider what people want to read.

Not sticking to your niche

Some bloggers suddenly branch out to other topics. This usually happens when they encounter writer's block or simply get bored of their current niche. By doing so, they ruin the specialization of the blog. As a result, the blog tends to be confusing and people will not know exactly what it is about.

If you want to branch out to a different niche, it would be better if you just open up an entirely new blog. To avoid the common problem of feeling like there is nothing left worth adding to your blog, you should avoid using a very specific name for your blog. For example, instead of a blog about the wonderful benefits of learning how to use a pendulum, your blog can be about divination, which encompasses subjects such as the use of a pendulum, tarot cards, numerology, and others. The drawback of using a less specific name is that it sacrifices specialization. Hence, there are advantages and disadvantages, and it all depends on your personal preference.

Conclusion

Thanks for making it through to the end of this book. We hope it was informative and provides you with all of the tools you need to achieve your goals whatever they may be.

The next step is to apply everything that you have learned. So, it is time to put up your own blog, start sharing, and rake in some serious profits.

Finally, if you found this book useful in any way, a review on Amazon is always appreciated!